MW01518458

THE CROWN

THE CROWN

By

Rabindranath Tagore

Translated into English by the Author

Introduction

Nirmal Kanti Bhattacharjee

**NIYOGI
BOOKS**

Published by

NIYOGI BOOKS
D-78, Okhla Industrial Area, Phase-I
New Delhi-110 020, INDIA
Tel: 91-11-26816301, 49327000
Fax: 91-11-26810483, 26813830
email: niyogibooks@gmail.com
website: www.niyogibooks.com

ISBN: 978-93-81523-25-4

Publication: 2012

Cover Design: Global Publishing Solutions, Noida
Printed at: Niyogi Offset Pvt. Ltd., New Delhi, India

Introduction

The Crown was originally published as a Bengali play called *Mukut* by Indian Publishing House in 1908 and was included in the *Rabindra Rachanavali* (Vol. 8) in 1941. Tagore himself translated it into English in 1918 under the title *The Crown*. We learn from the diary of Rabhindranath Tagore that: "The way he did this was to take the Bengali book in his hand and dictate the translation in English to Mr. Andrews who put it down to paper." However, the English translation, though repeatedly retouched and improved by Tagore, was never published in his life-time. It is only in 1983 that it was first published in the *Rabindra-Biksha* (Issue 9) and later collected in *The English Writings of Rabindranath Tagore* (Vol. Two), edited by Sisir Kumar Das and published by Sahitya Akademi in 1996.

The Crown is a narrative drama in three Acts. The Act I contains three scenes, while Act II has six and Act III only three scenes. Designed to be enacted by the boy students of the Brahmacharyashram school of Bolpur, the play shows the defeat of falsehood and meanness at the hands of truth and greatness of heart. Based on an episode of the royal family of the princely state of Tripura, the play has three main characters—wily youngest prince Rajdhar, heroic middle prince Indrakumar and the loving eldest prince and heir-apparent Chandramanikya. The play dramatizes the conflict between the three princes with the crown at the centre of dispute. The cunning youngest prince Rajdhar earned for himself the crown from the enemy through lies and deceit, but he did not dare to brag his costly victory before the greatness of the dying braveheart prince Chandramanikya. The quality of mind and heart has been given predominance over that of might and intelligence. The one who is pure of heart ultimately wins the crown, although in the apparent battle of life it might look as if he has lost. This loss is only apparent because he wins not a country but the heart of crores of people.

The Crown is purposefully devoid of any women characters so that the boys of the school find it easy to stage. Unlike many of Tagore's other plays, it is totally bereft of any song or symbolism. Although confined to aristocracy and a limited way of life, the play nevertheless does not lack in dramatic action. Not just the excitement of the battlefield but the fiery conflicts of heart also make the play bright and dazzling. General Isha Khan and the three princes reveal their identity and character through brief but scintillating dialogues in the very first two-three scenes. Behind Isha Khan's self-respect and uninhibited straight talks lies his sense of justice and love for his worthy disciple, the eldest prince Chandramanikya. The eldest prince admires the heroism of the middle prince on one side and indulges in the caprices of the much-maligned youngest prince on the other. He acts as an apostle of peace between the two erupting volcanoes of the royal family and often sacrifices his own rights on the altar of familial compromise. Although Indrakumar is the epitome of an ideal Kshatriya hero, he is too sensitive to minor family issues and extremely impatient of Rajdhar's mean tricks. It is Indrakumar's arrogance and constant indictment of Rajdhar which might have pushed the latter to the extreme path of treason.

The end of the play, however, does not do justice to Tagore's reputation as a playwright. As a repentant Indrakumar who had forsaken his elder brother out of anger, begs forgiveness of the dying Chandramanikya, Rajdhar enters the scene and places the ill-earned crown at the feet of Chandramanikya, who directs him to offer it to Indrakumar. Indrakumar in turn again places the crown on Rajdhar's head. The whole situation smacks of sentimentalism. Moreover, there was no preparation for the mental metamorphosis of Rajdhar. Hence, his repentance does not rise to the level of credibility, leaving the readers/audience somewhat sceptic and confused.

—*Nirmal Kanti Bhattacharjee*

ACT I SCENE 1

The First Trial
The Tournament

Chamber of **Ishah Khan,** *the General of Tipperah.*
Ishah Khan *is seen engaged in cleaning his weapons,*
while the youngest Prince of Tipperah, **Rajdhar,**
is speaking to him.

Rajdhar.	I warn you once more. General, do not call me by my name.
Ishah Khan.	Then how must I call you,—by pulling your ear?
Rajdhar.	If you don't pay me respect, I shall repay yon in your own coin.

Ishah Khan.	If my respect were at your disposal, I would go and sell it in the market for a brass farthing. I can better look after my own position myself.
Rajdhar.	If you wish to do that, then don't call me by my name in future.
Ishah Khan.	Indeed!
Rajdhar.	Yes!
Ishah Khan [*laughs aloud*].	Then how am I to call Your Highness? Shall I call you my Lord,—or my Master, or your Excellency?
Rajdhar.	I may be your pupil,—yet I am a Prince! You must not forget that.
Ishah Khan.	If I did forget it, then it was because you made it hard for me to remember.
Rajdhar.	You are also making it hard for me to remember that you are my Tutor.
Ishah Khan.	Silence! Have done!

Enter the Second Prince, Indrakumar.

Indrakumar.   Khan Sahib, what is all this noise?

Ishah Khan.   Listen to this! This young man here, who is the youngest of you all, imagines that unless he is called King of Kings and Emperor of Emperors his honour will be insulted. He is in such desperate straits about, it!

Indrakumar.   Really? [*Laughs aloud.*]

Rajdhar.   Stop that laughing.

Indrakumar.   Pray how must we call you?—Your Majesty [*Laughs.*]—Your Imperial Highness? [*Laughs again*]

Rajdhar.   I tell you again,—Silence.

Indrakumar.   Your Highness!—[*Laughs.*] Oh, I can't contain myself—Your Majesty!—[*Laughs out loud.*] Oh, I shall break my sides with laughter.

Rajdhar.   Fool!

Indrakumar.   Keep your temper, Rajdhar! Keep your

wisdom to yourself. I have no wish to
deprive you of any of it.

Ishah Khan.   His wisdom of late has grown
too exalted.

Indrakumar.   Yes, Khan Sahib, it has grown quite out
of reach. It would take a ladder to climb
up to it.

Enter Maharajah Amar, *of Tipperah,* **and the
Jubaraj,** *(the Heir Apparent)* **Chandrakumar
with Attendants.**

Rajdhar.   Sire, I have a complaint to make to you.

Maharajah.   What is it, Rajdhar?

Rajdhar.   In spite of repeated warnings, Ishah Khan
takes every occasion to insult me, I ask
for your protection.

Ishah Khan.   The source of your insult is not anyone
outside; it is in yourself. There are other
princes besides you. They always bear
in mind that I am their tutor, and I also
know that they are my pupils, and so there
arises no question of honour or insult.

Maharajah.	General, the Princes are grown up. We should be careful to pay them proper respect.
Ishah Khan.	Maharajah, time was, when you yourself were my pupil. I cannot treat these Princes with greater respect that I did you.
Rajdhar.	I have nothing to say about others but—
Ishah Khan.	Child, silence! I am talking to your father.—Maharajah, pardon me if I forget myself! I am obliged to tell you that this youngest scion of your House may in time become expert in wielding his pen, but he will never take to the sword. [*Pointing to the Jubaraj and second prince*] Look at these, Maharajah— those are true Princes.
Maharajah.	Rajdhar, have you failed to satisfy your Tutor in your bouts at arms?
Rajdhar.	If that is true, then my fate is to blame rather than my skill. I ask you to hold a Tournament in archery tomorrow.

Maharajah.	Very well. Tomorrow we have leisure, and we shall test your skill. Whoever wins in the Tournament shall have this jewelled sword of mine.

[*Maharajah departs.*]

Ishah Khan.	Well said, Rajdhar, well spoken! For once you have spoken as the son of a Kshatriya should speak. Even if you are defeated, it will not be inglorious. Victory and defeat are in the hands of Allah.
Rajdhar.	Have done, General, keep your praises for the other Princes. If I could do without them so long, I can do without them now.
Jubaraj.	Don't be angry with the General. If you win in this Tournament, then the reward you get from the Khan Sahib will exceed that from all others.
Rajdhar.	Tonight is the full moon. What do you say to going out to shoot tigers at the place where they come to drink at the Gomati River?
Jubaraj.	Excellent.

Indrakumar.	This is astonishing!—Rajdhar shooting tigers! Hunting is not in his line.
Ishah Khan.	Not in his line? Why he hunts the greater game! There is scarcely a single two footed animal in the King's Court who has never been snared in his noose.
Jubaraj.	General your sword and your tongue are both terribly keen. They never return without piercing the heart.
Rajdhar.	Don't pity me, Jubaraj! Let Khan Sahib whet his tongue into a knife, if he likes. It will never leave a scratch in my heart.
Indrakumar.	Who can reach your heart? That is difficult indeed.
Jubaraj.	Indrakumar, you are getting into the habit of hurting Rajdhar at every turn.
Rajdhar.	And I have got into the habit of not getting hurt by anything he says.
Indrakumar.	Have you really made up your mind to go out hunting?

Jubaraj.	But, Indrakumar, it is quite useless for us to go hunting when you are one of the party, because then for us it becomes a ridiculously vegetarian affair! While you get all the big game in the forest, we have to be content to fill our hunting bags with gourds.
Ishah Khan [*slapping Indrakumar on the back*].	The Jubaraj is right, who can compete with you?
Indrakumar [*to the Jubaraj*]	No. No. Joking apart, you must come with us.
Jubaraj.	Very well, I will come.

[*They go out. Enter Attendants.*]

1st Attendant.	It sounds suspicious, Our youngest Prince is no adept in archery. Everyone knows that. Yet, what is the meaning of his challenging our second Prince?
2nd Attendant.	Some reach their aim with arrows, and some with cunning.
1st Attendant.	Yes, that is the thing to be feared. When it is a trial of skill in the Tournament, if

cunning is used instead of archery, it is an evil thing.

3rd Attendant. Look here, Bansi, let them use archery or cunning just as they like—but you had better keep a wise tongue in your head, if you want to live quietly, that's my advice.

2nd Attendant. Yet, Bonomali is quite right. Bansi, you become quite wild in your talk when you speak of the youngest Prince. It is not for us to judge the respective merits of the Princes,—only we can pray that our Jubaraj may live long, that our second Prince may guard him from all mischief, and as for our youngest Prince, let us keep silence.

1st Attendant. Our second Prince is absolutely simple. He has neither fear in his mind, nor crookedness in his nature. Our fear is that the one, whom we need not name, may lead him into trouble at any moment.

2nd Attendant. Ah! There they come. Let us go away.

1st Attendant. His cousin Dhurandhar comes with him. It's like the evil planet, Mars, in conjunction with the planet Saturn.

[*They go out. Enter Rajdhar and Dhurandhar.*]

Rajdhar. It is intolerable.

Dhurandhar. I see no sign of your tolerance wearing out. This friction has been going on almost from your birth, but it is not yet clear that the situation has become intolerable.

Rajdhar. It will be quite clear, when the time comes. I am going to get my chance. In this Tournament I shall hit the mark.

Dhurandhar. Where is your target? In Indrakumar's breast?

Rajdhar. Not his breast, but his heart. This time I shall win and pierce his pride through and through.

Dhurandhar. You expect to beat Indrakumar, and call this your opportunity?

Rajdhar. Opportunity is not always on the point of the arrow. But you must help me.

Dhurandhar.   I have been helping you all along, but it has led to no result.

Rajdhar.   Results ripen in time. You must get access to Indrakumar's room, where he keeps his arrows, and substitute my arrows for his in his quiver. With this change of arrows will come a change of destinies.

Dhurandhar.   That is quite a simple thing to do, but what about my life? That cannot be exchanged.

Rajdhar.   Have no fear. I am behind you.

Dhurandhar.   You may be there behind me, but fear is there also. Do you remember when you desired to have the bow with the silver chasing belonging to Indrakumar? I got it for you and kept it hidden in your room, but when it was discovered at last, Indrakumar contemptuously made it a present to you but the insult which came to my share I shall never forget all my life. You were there also behind me,— very much behind.

Rajdhar.   The time has come for you to take your own vengeance.

Dhurandhar. Yes, the time may have come, but it is difficult to divine for whom it has arrived. The best thing for weak people is to have a strong digestion for insults. Revenge may be too dangerous a luxury.

[*They go out talking.*]

ACT I SCENE 2

Door of Indrakumar's weapon-room.

Enter* Indrakumar *and* Pratap, *an Attendant.

Indrakumar. What is it, Pratap? Why have you called me here.

Pratap. Her highness asked me to tell you that a living weapon has entered your room by some chance or other. One should make due investigation about its nature.

Indrakumar. What do you say, Pratap? Does such a thing happen even in this Iron Age?

Pratap. Yes, Prince. Only in the Iron Age can such

a thing be made possible. Open the door and you will understand everything.

Indrakumar.   Indeed, I hear footsteps inside! [*The door is opened and Rajdhar comes out.*] What is this, Rajdhar? [*Laughs.*] Has any stupid servant of mine mistaken you for some weapon? [*Laughs loudly.*]

Rajdhar.   My sister-in-law played practical joke on me and kept me captive.

Indrakumar.   This is not a room for dull, ordinary jokes. The jokes kept, here are uncommonly sharp.

Rajdhar.   I found out that most of my own arrows were rusty and not fit of the shooting party tonight. I have sent them to be cleaned for tomorrow's Tournament and that is why I came to borrow arrows from our sister-in-law.

Indrakumar.   Is that why she has lent you the whole room? [*Laughs aloud.*]

Rajdhar [*aside*]. You may have your laugh now, but this joke will bring me my share of the laughter,—but not now.... I take me leave. I am not going out to the shooting party tonight.

[*He goes out.*]

Pratap. I do not think, Sir, it was wise to jest with our youngest Prince.

[*They go out together.*]

ACT I SCENE 3

The Palace of Tourney.
Enter the royal princes, **Ishah Khan** *and others.*

Indrakumar
[to Jubaraj].

You must win. Otherwise it won't do!

Jubaraj.

Who can say it won't do? Even if my arrow misses its mark, the world will go on just as it did before; and if it doesn't, yet I do not see any chance of my winning?

Indrakumar.

If you miss your aim, then I shall miss mine on purpose.

Jubaraj.

Don't be childish. You must keep up the reputation of your Tutor.

Ishah Khan. Jubaraj the time has come. Take your bow. Aim carefully. Steady! Now!

[*The Jubaraj shoots.*]

Ishah Khan. Missed!

Jubaraj. I fixed my mind, but I failed to fix my arrow.

Indrakumar. I can't believe it; If you had put your mind into it, I am sure you would have won. It gives me real pain when I find that by sheer apathy you miss your chance.

Ishah Khan. Do you know why your brother's intelligence does not shine at the point of an arrow. It is because it is blunt.

Indrakumar. General, you do him an injustice.

Ishah Khan [*to Rajdhar*]. Prince, now it is your turn. Maharajah, watch.

Rajdhar. Indrakumar must precede me.

Ishah Khan [*angrily*].	Do what I tell you.

[*Rajdhar shoots.*]

Ishah Khan.	Missed!
Jubaraj.	Rajdhar, you have just missed by a hair's breadth.
Rajdhar [*excitedly*].	No. I have not missed! You cannot see it plainly at this distance.
Jubaraj.	No, Rajdhar, you are mistaken. Your arrow has not hit the mark.
Rajdhar.	You have a prejudice against me, that is why you say it. We shall see when we examine at close quarters.

[*Indrakumar takes up his bow.*]

Jubaraj.	I am useless. But do not be vexed with me, Indrakumar, for that. If your arrow misses its aim, then it will pierce my heart,—be sure of that.

[*Indrakumar shoots.*]

The Spectators. Victory to Indrakumar!

Ishah Khan.   My son, may Allah give you long life. Maharajah, Indrakumar has won the prize.

Rajdhar.   No, Sir! The prize is mine. It is my arrow that pierced the mark.

Maharajah.   No, that cannot be.

Rajdhar.   General, go and examine and see whose arrow it is that is in the mark.

Ishah Khan.   I will go.
                    [*He comes back with the arrow.*]

Ishah Khan   I am an old man. Is it possible that I
[to Indrakumar]   read the letters wrongly? The name, engraved on this arrow, seems to be that of Rajdhar.

Indrakumar.   Yes, it is his name.

Maharajah.   Let me see. Well,—how is it we all made the same mistake?

Rajdhar.   This mistake did not start from today; it has been going on for a long while.

Ishah Khan.	I do not understand.
Indrakumar.	But I do.
Rajdhar.	Maharajah, Give judgment,
Indrakumar [*aside to Rajdhar*].	You ask for judgment! If judgment is visited upon you, your head will be bowed to the dust. But I shall not speak a word. God will judge you.
Ishah Khan.	What is the matter? There is some mystery behind it.—It is as difficult to believe that stones float in water and monkeys sink [*sing*]. Indrakumar, tell me truly, has there been no misplacement of arrows in the quiver?
Rajdhar.	Never! Examine that for yourself.
Ishah Khan [*examining*].	Yes, the quivers are all right. Do you know if any one had access to your weapon-room lately?
Indrakumar.	General, let the subject drop.
Ishah Khan.	Then you accept defeat?

Indrakumar.   Yes.

Ishah Khan.   Well done, lad, I always felt that there was some wrong somewhere. But it remains obscure. Unless we have another Tournament it will not clear up.

Rajdhar.   There is no other wrong, except my winning. But I am not going to put up with the insult of a second trial. If you think it was unfair for me to win, let the prize go to Indrakumar. I refuse to take it.

Maharajah.   To that I cannot agree. When the arrow bears your name I am bound to give the prize to you. Here is the sword.

Rajdhar.   I take it, with all due respect. But since I find that it offends every one, I give up my sword to Indrakumar.

[*He holds it out to Indrakumar. Indrakumar flings it to the ground.*]

Indrakumar.   Who is going to take a prize from your hand?

Ishah Khan [*taking hold of Indrakumar's hand*].	Indrakumar! How dare you insult the Maharajah, by throwing his sword on the ground. You must be punished for this.
Indrakumar. [*snatching his hand away*].	Old man! Don't touch me.
Ishah Khan.	My son! You forget yourself.
Indrakumar.	General, forgive me. I forgot myself. Punish me.
Jubaraj.	Peace, let us return.
Indrakumar [*making obeisance to the Maharajah*].	Father, pardon me for my insolence. To-day my defeat has been complete.
Ishah Khan.	Maharajah, I have another request to make to you. This Tournament is over but that is mere play. Let a trail at arms be held in the proper field.

Maharajah.   Ishah Khan, do you lead these Princes to
                 the field, and may heaven protect them!

ACT II SCENE 1

Maharajah.   What field is that for Indrakumar, General?

Ishah Khan.   Your intention was to fight against the Rajah of Arakan. The soldiers are ready. Let our Princes take part in this fight.

Maharajah.   That is well said. I have heard that the Rajah of Arakan has come very near to the boundaries of Chittagong. He had, a while ago, repeated lessons. But the fool was never contented; nor will he be, until he has his final lesson in death. What do you say, children? Are you ready to test your manhood on the battle-field?

Indrakumar.	Yes, I am; and I am sure that the Jubaraj will come also. Rajdhar. And do you suppose that I shall remain behind?

The Second Trial
The Battle Field
SCENE 1
Rajdhar's Camp

***Enter* Rajdhar *and* Dhurandhar.**

Dhurandhar.	You say that you will remain apart with your five thousand soldiers.
Rajdhar.	Yes. I sent this proposal to Ishah Khan.
Dhurandhar.	I know that, because I was present there, and they had a long talk about it.
Rajdhar.	What they say?
Dhurandhar.	At the very outset Indrakumar laughed aloud. He said 'Rajdhar has his own peculiar way of fighting; his warfare takes place far away from the battle-field.'

Rajdhar.   Well, he was right. Thou who fight in the field are mere labourers. He who can fight from a distance is the real warrior.

Dhurandhar.   You know how little he trusts you. If you go near to touch his feet he suspects that you are going to steal his shoes, Ishah Khan said,—'It is nothing very wonderful for Rajdhar to wish to be far away from battle-field; but I do not like his keeping those five thousand soldiers to himself.'

Rajdhar.   Did the Jubaraj say nothing?

Dhurandhar.   The Jubaraj! God has not spared him even that one spark of intelligence which is required to suspect anybody. Even you he can trust!

Rajdhar.   Be careful what you say, Dhurandhar. You must not talk about the Jubaraj like that.

Dhurandhar.   I understand. You have a tender spot somewhere, which I forget now and

then. However, the Jubaraj said,—
'No, you are doing an injustice to
Rajdhar. His proposal seems to me to
be a wise one. If any crisis comes in
the war he will be able to help us with
his reserves.'—Ishah Khan only gave
his consent, after being induced to do
so by the Jubaraj,—though, even then,
he had his misgivings. However, I do
not fully understand your intention of
keeping aloof.

Rajdhar. It is because I do not see any profit in
joining with them in this battle; because
in case of victory no one would give me
the least credit for it.

Dhurandhar. But yet, by some mistake perhaps,
people may mention you; while, if
you are absent, you will get no credit
whether they win or lose.

Rajdhar. But I tell you, I shall win!

Enters Messenger.

Rajdhar. What is the news.

Messenger.	The battle is going on. But our side has not yet been able to pierce the enemy's line. The sun is about to set and I expect that the battle will close for the day.

Enters Second Messenger.

Rajdhar.	Who are you?
Second Messenger.	My name is Bhola [Byomkesh]. The Jubaraj sent me about three hours ago: but, because you have moved from the place where you had your camp, it has taken all this time to find you out.
Rajdhar.	What is his wish?
Second Messenger.	The fight has become very hard indeed. Prince Indrakumar, with his cavalry, had attacked the enemy from the North. If he had had a little more time he could easily have driven them to the brink of the river.

Rajdhar
[somewhat
sarcastically]. Really! What is the use of guessing what might have happened, if he had had a little more time? The important thing seems to be that he never had the time.

Second When the enemy was very nearly

Messenger. wavering Indrakumar heard that the Jubaraj was in difficulties, surrounded by the enemy, while Ishah Khan was engaged in some other part of the field. When Ishah Khan learnt this he said, 'I have not come here to save the Jubaraj but to win the battle. I cannot stir from this place.'

Rajdhar. Then, is the Jubaraj—

Second No, he is out of danger. Indrakumar

Messenger. went to his help and because of that things have gone wrong. Messengers have been sent out in all directions to search for you. If you do not come to our help, the battle will be lost.

Rajdhar.	I shall not delay.
Dhurandhar.	Are you going to move forward? [*The two Messengers depart.*]
Rajdhar.	Yes but in another direction.
Dhurandhar.	Do you mean towards home?
Rajdhar.	Have you also taken your lesson in sarcasm from Ishah Khan? Let those who will show their bravery, but if any one retires home victorious, it will be myself. Dhurandhar, go and see that all the lights are extinguished in my camp.
Dhurandhar.	Tell me frankly what is your intention. If you distrust me and I distrust you,— then, for us two there will remain no place in this wide world.
Rajdhar.	I shall secretly cross the river with my soldiers under cover of darkness. I want to surprise the Rajah of Arakan in his camp and capture him.

Dhurandhar.   But how can you manage to cross without any landing-place?

Rajdhar.   I have reconnoitered. The sun has set; the moon will rise at about one o'clock at night and we must finish our work before that. Time is short; we must get ready.

ACT II SCENE 2

Ishah Khan's Camp

Enter **Indrakumar** *and* **Ishah Khan.**

Indrakumar.   General, do not be angry with the Jubaraj. Let our soldiers take rest tonight. Tomorrow we shall win.

Ishah Khan.   Indrakumar, you ought to understand that a fire must be put out without delay. If you give it time to spread, it may get beyond control. We should have won the battle today, but your brother like a fool entangled himself for nothing and ruined everything.

Indrakumar.   Why do you say 'like a fool'. Why

don't you say 'like a brave man'. With only a handful of soldiers, he—

Ishah Khan. He got into a place where only fools can go.

Indrakumar. No! Only the bravest would dare to enter there—

Ishah Khan. Very well, let it be so. Let us say that only a brave man, who is a fool withal, could get into that situation.

Indrakumar. But that did not interfere with your plans.

Ishah Khan. Yes it did! because all our soldiers got anxious and lost heart. We have not got a single man in our army who could remain unmoved at the news of any danger coming to the Jubaraj.

Indrakumar. But, General, what is the news about Rajdhar.

Ishah Khan. I have sent messengers in all directions but he cannot be found.

Indrakumar [*laughs*].	He must have run away.
Ishah Khan.	It is no laughing matter.
Indrakumar.	Well, I confess, I feel glad. I could never bear it,—to share our fame with him when we have won, though he did nothing to help us. It is a good thing that he has fled. This time, in the trial of the battle-field cunning would not—
Ishah Khan.	You never told me what really happened at the Tournament.
Indrakumar.	Don't ask me, General. I own that I was defeated.

ACT II SCENE 3

Camp of the Rajah of Arakan

Enter **Rajah of Arakan** *and* **Rajdhar.**

Arakan.   Prince, it will not profit you keep me captive.

Rajdhar.   Why, Sire? To gain you is the greatest profit of this war.

Arakan.   This will not end the war. My brother, Hamchu, is still living. The soldiers will crown him, and the battle will continue.

Rajdhar.   I will set you free; but your freedom must have its price.

Arakan.   That I know. I am willing to sign the conditions of peace, acknowledging my defeat to you.

Rajdhar.   No mere signing will do, Rajah, I must have some tangible proofs of your defeat to take home.

Arakan.   You shall have five hundred Burmese horses from me and three elephants.

Rajdhar.   No, I must take your royal crown.

Arakan.   You may take my crown, but understand that along with my crown you are taking away the undying enmity of Arakan's royal house. So long as this crown remains with you there will be no peace.

Rajdhar.   Peace we do not desire, Rajah. We are Kshatriyas.—One duty still remains to be done. Send a letter signed by yourself to the battle-field, commanding your General to stop the battle.

ACT II SCENE 4

The Field of Battle

The **Jubaraj** *and* **Indrakumar.**

Jubaraj.　　It is difficult to know which side is going to win. It seems to me that our soldiers are still despondent. They are not putting forth all their strength. Where is Ishah Khan?

Indrakumar.　You can see his flag in the East.

Jubaraj.　　Why do you follow me today? I think you ought to go to the North.

Indrakumar.　No, this is my proper place.

Jubaraj.	Indrakumar, you are trying to save your brother from committing any folly. You cannot bear that the General should blame me for another blunder. But you must understand that there are limitations even to my foolishness, and possibly I shall be able to act with more circumspection today. But look—what is that?—It doesn't seem to be right! Our soldiers are already beginning to waver on the left. They may take to flight. Indrakumar, go and try to hold them. Don't be afraid about my safety. But what!—What is this? What can be the meaning of it all?
Indrakumar.	I cannot understand why the enemy should stop the fight so suddenly.
Jubaraj.	They have hoisted the flag of peace. But there was no cause for this, for they have been winning up to now.

***Enters* Messenger.**

Messenger.	Sire, the enemy has stopped the battle.

Jubaraj.	For what reason?
Messenger.	We do not know the reason, but we have heard that the Rajah of Arakan has sent word that he will no longer fight with us.
Jubaraj.	That is good news! But there is something that pains me.
Indrakumar.	What?
Jubaraj.	Why did Rajdhar keep away with his soldiers? If only he were by our side then, we three brothers would have held the Festival of Victory together. His absence from us leaves a great gap in our glory.
Indrakumar.	What harm is there, if he has fled, without claiming his share in the battle?
Jubaraj.	The General is coming this way riding on his horse.

Enters **Ishah Khan.**

Indrakumar.	General, why did the enemy stop so suddenly. Have you got the news?
Ishah Khan.	Yes! Rajdhar has captured the Rajah of Arakan!
Indrakumar.	Rajdhar! That cant be true!
Ishah Khan.	Sometimes things, that ought to have been false, become true. I find that Allah's messengers occasionally go to sleep and Satan takes that opportunity to falsify the accounts.
Indrakumar.	But could ever Satan help Rajdhar to win?
Ishah Khan.	Don't you remember that Tournament— how the Devil helped him. The same Devil has helped him in this battle.
Jubaraj	General, do not be angry with Rajdhar if he has won! It is our victory. But when did it happen?

Ishah Khan.	Yesterday, when we had retired from the field, in the evening he secretly crossed the river and captured the Rajah of Arakan in his camp. I had sent word to him to get ready to join us. But he had already shifted his place and had disobeyed my orders.
Indrakumar.	Intolerable! He ought to be punished for this.
Ishah Khon.	Not only so, but he has drawn up a peace document on his own initiative, without waiting for the Jubaraj!
Indrakumar.	He must be punished for that!
Ishah Khan.	Do explain this very simple matter to your elder brother.

Enters *Rajdhar*.

Indrakumar.	Rajdhar, you have displayed cowardice!
Rajdhar.	I did not come here to display my

bravery like you by spoiling the battle. I came to win it.

Indrakumar. You won the battle! You won It! You have made the Goddess of Victory blush.

Rajdhar. Yes, blush with the shyness of love. This is the sign that she has accepted me.   [*Holds up the crown.*]

Indrakumar. Whose crown is that?

Rajdhar. It is mine. It is the prize that I have got in this war.

Indrakumar. You who kept away from the battle,—a prize for you! No! This crown is for the Jubaraj.

Jubaraj. Rajdhar is right. The crown belongs to him.

Ishah Khan. He who shrank away from my command in the dark can never claim the prize.

Rajdhar.	I should like to know, if I had not been here, what kind of a crown would have awaited you by this time and where you would all be?
Indrakumar.	Wherever we might be, it is certain that we should not have kept hiding!
Jubaraj.	Indrakumar, you are unjust. The truth is that Rajdhar had not been here, we should be in danger today.
Indrakumar.	Danger! No danger whatever!—Danger there was, because he kept away our soldiers. If Rajdhar had not been here, I would have got this crown fighting honestly and openly,—He has stolen it like a thief. And then, further, I would have brought this crown to you. I would never have claimed it for myself.
Jubaraj.	Rajdhar, you have won the victory today. Let me crown you.
Indrakumar [*with a choking voice*].	You—you crown him! You crown Rajdhar because he was dishonoured his knighthood. And I,—I, who was

	ready to sacrifice my life to save you, never get a single word of praise from you. Oh, that I should live to hear you say that if Rajdhar had not been there, nobody could have helped you!
Jubaraj.	Indrakumar, I never spoke of my own danger.
Indrakumar.	Enough, enough! Now that you have got such a fine ally on your side, you have no need of me, and I depart.
Jubaraj.	Brother, you are again forgetting yourself—
Indrakumar.	It is a disgrace to remain, where one is not needed.

[*He goes away.*]

Ishah Khan.	Jubaraj, you have no right to offer this crown to anybody. I am the General in this battle, It is at my disposal.

[*He is about to put it on the Jubaraj's head.*]

Jubaraj.	No, I cannot accept this.

Ishah Khan.	Then no one else must have the crown: let it go into the river. Rajdhar has violated the laws of war and he deserved punishment.

[*Throws the crown into the river.*]

Rajdhar.	Brother, you are my witness. I shall never forget this.

Jubaraj.	Do you think that this is the one fact to be remembered above all others? If the crown has disappeared in the water let all shame attached to it disappear at the same moment. Do you on your part forget what you must, and let us forget what we should. Let me go and see if Indrakumar has left in anger.

[*Ishah Khan and Jubaraj go out.*]

ACT II SCENE 5

***Enters* Dhurandhar**.

Rajdhar. Dhurandhar, I will offer as a sacrifice this my victor to the River, Karnafuli where my crown has vanished.

Dhurandhar. Do you mean to be defeated again?

Rajdhar. Yes, I will win through my defeat. I shall not return home till I bring Indrakumar's pride to the dust. He would not accept victory at my hands; let me see if he can earn it himself.

Dhurandhar. Don't be too certain. He may win by chance.—It is no use being angry with

me for telling the truth. Indrakumar
knows the art of warfare.

Rajdhar.   We shall argue that out later. Meanwhile
you have to do me a service. Arakan
is going to start for his own country
tomorrow morning. As long as he is on
this side of the Chittagong boundary,
all his officers will remain hostages in
my camp. You have to take a message
of mine to him tonight.

Dhurandhar.   What message?

Rajdhar.   Tell him that I have been insulted, and
therefore I have seceded. I will pretend
that I am taking my departure home with
my five thousand soldiers. Indrakumar
has already left in a fit of passion. The
soldiers are getting ready to go home,
knowing that the battle is over. If the
Rajah of Arakan takes this opportunity
to attack them, then Chittagong will
be defeated.

Dhurandhar.   Yes, they will be defeated,—
but what then? If you must set fire

to other people's houses, take care of your own.

Rajdhar. I have never been suspected of being a fool. So I need no advice from you.

ACT II SCENE 6

The Field of Battle

Enter **Ishah Khan** *and* **Jubaraj.**

Ishah Khan.   Jubaraj, call upon Allah. The times are difficult.

Jubaraj.   Why, Khan Sahib, when Allah wills it, it is neither difficult to live nor to die.

Ishah Khan.   Because the Maharajah was confident in my strength he put you in my charge and only that troubles me. Jubaraj, try to save yourself and leave the battle to me.

Jubaraj.   My tutor, this advice does not become

you,—and further, the roads are all
closed. Death's opportunity has become
an easier one than that of flight.

Ishah Khan.   Jubaraj, a fire is burning in my heart.
The one regret that rankles in my
mind is this, that I shall probably not
live to punish Indrakumar for having
deserted us.

Jubaraj.   If you do not live, General, his
punishment will be all the greater. He
loves you as his Father.

Ishah Khan.   Allah! That is true!—Jubaraj, I know that
I shall not have time, but if you have the
opportunity, tell him that if Ishah Khan
had lived, he would have punished him;
but he forgives him before he dies. No
more! The time is up. I take my leave.
Let me embrace you! I leave you in the
hands of Allah. He will save you.

Jubaraj.   Khan Sahib, I ask for your forgiveness
for any wrong I might have done you.

ACT III SCENE 1

The Reward
The Battle-field

Enter Soldiers.

1st Soldier.   Is it true?

2nd Soldier.   Yes, that is what I have heard.

1st Soldier.   What a terrible misfortune!
    [*They go out. Another group enters.*]

1st Soldier.   Who told you?

2nd Soldier.   Our Umesh.

3rd Soldier.   It stunned me completely and I could

not ask him all the details.
[*They go out. A third group enters.*]

1st Soldier.   We have seen his elephant, but it had not howdah and mahut. It is wandering about wildly without its master.

2nd Soldier.   We are in the same condition. Has no one seen where he has fallen?

1st Soldier.   No, nobody seems to know it.

2nd Soldier.   But our Shibu said that when the arrow struck the Jubaraj, the driver was running away with the elephant and the driver got killed. After the Jubaraj was struck with the arrow the mahut tried to drive the elephant out of the battle, and then the driver himself got killed, and after that nobody knows where the Jubaraj fell.
[*They go out. Enter a fourth group.*]

1st Soldier.   After this calamity, is there no one who can take this news to Prince Indrakumar?

2nd *Soldier.* Yes, messengers have been sent, but we don't know if they have found him.

3rd *Soldier.* Has not Prince Rajdhar heard this news?

2nd *Soldier.* I think he has started for Tipperah. Surely he would have come back to help the Jubaraj, if he had known it.

1st Soldier. How can we return home?

3rd *Soldier.* Why return?—I shall die.
                                              [*Enters a Man.*]

Man. Why, what are you doing? Come and let us seek him.

1st Soldier. Let us go in different directions.
[*Exeunt.*]

ACT III SCENE 2

***Enter* Indrakumar *and a* Soldier.**

Indrakumar.   Where, where,—where is my brother?

Soldier.   We are seeking for him.

Indrakumar.   And where is Ishah Khan?

Soldier.   To-day, before the fourth watch, the Jubaraj with his own hand heaped earth on the grave of Ishah Khan and his own blood was mingled with that earth.

Indrakumar.   Oh, shame, shame, shame to my anger! My brother, will you not grant me one moment to ask your forgiveness.

***Enters* 2nd Soldier.**

2nd Soldier.	Prince, come this way, we have found him.
Indrakumar.	Where?
2nd Soldier.	On the bank of the Karnaphuli river, under that Arjun tree.
Indrakumar.	Tell me truly, is he still—

[*They go out.*]

ACT III SCENE 3

On the bank of the Karnaphuli.

Jubaraj.   Move that branch aside a little, let me see the moon. Ah!—Nobody near me?—Is that the shadow of the tree? Or is it the shadow of death? —I can still hear the murmur of the water. Is that the last farewell greeting of the earth to me? Indrakumar, my darling brother, are you still keeping away in anger?

***Enters* Indrakumar.**

Indrakumar.   My brother!

Jubaraj.   Ah, what peace! I knew you would

come, and that kept me alive so long! You parted from me in anger, and I could not die without seeing you.

Other Classics in the Tagore Series

- The King of the Dark Chamber
- Fireflies
- Fruit Gathering
- Gitanjali
- Malini
- Nationalism
- Red Oleanders
- Religion of Man
- Sacrifice
- The Crescent Moon
- The Fugitive